Table of Contents

Part I – About OGE

Mission Statement

The United States Office of Government Ethics (OGE) provides overall leadership and oversight of the executive branch ethics program designed to prevent and resolve conflicts of interest. OGE's mission directly supports the President's goal of responsibly governing the nation.

Background

OGE was established by the Ethics in Government Act of 1978. To carry out its leadership and oversight responsibilities over the executive branch ethics program, OGE promulgates and maintains enforceable standards of ethical conduct for approximately 2.7 million civilian employees in over 130 executive branch agencies and the White House; oversees a financial disclosure system that reaches more than 28,000 public and 325,000 confidential financial disclosure report filers; ensures that executive branch ethics programs are in compliance with applicable ethics laws and regulations; provides education and training to the more than 5,600 ethics officials executive branch-wide; conducts outreach to the general public, the private sector, and civil society; and shares model practices with state, local, and foreign governments, and international organizations.

OGE's greatest resource is its multi-disciplinary staff of attorneys, ethics and financial experts, and support staff. OGE is a lean organization, with approximately 80 full-time equivalents, and accomplishes its responsibilities by organizing cross-functional teams to perform such diverse tasks as working with Presidential nominees for appointments requiring Senate confirmation to resolve potential financial conflicts of interest, training executive branch ethics officials, and enhancing oversight of executive branch ethics programs.

Part II – Fiscal Year 2013 Performance Highlights

In fiscal year 2013, the last year under OGE's prior strategic plan, OGE advanced its strategic goals of strengthening the ethical culture within the executive branch, preventing conflicts of interest, and promoting good governance. OGE advanced each of the strategic goals by focusing on the following three priorities:

1. Interpreting, implementing, and advising on government ethics laws, policies, and program management;

2. Harnessing technology to promote transparency, education, and oversight; and

3. Ensuring effective communications to enhance understanding of government ethics laws, policies, and program management, and to promote transparency, education, and oversight.

OGE's fiscal year 2013 strategic goals and priorities, as well as the strategic objectives that OGE identified in order to achieve its priorities, are depicted in Figure 1 below.

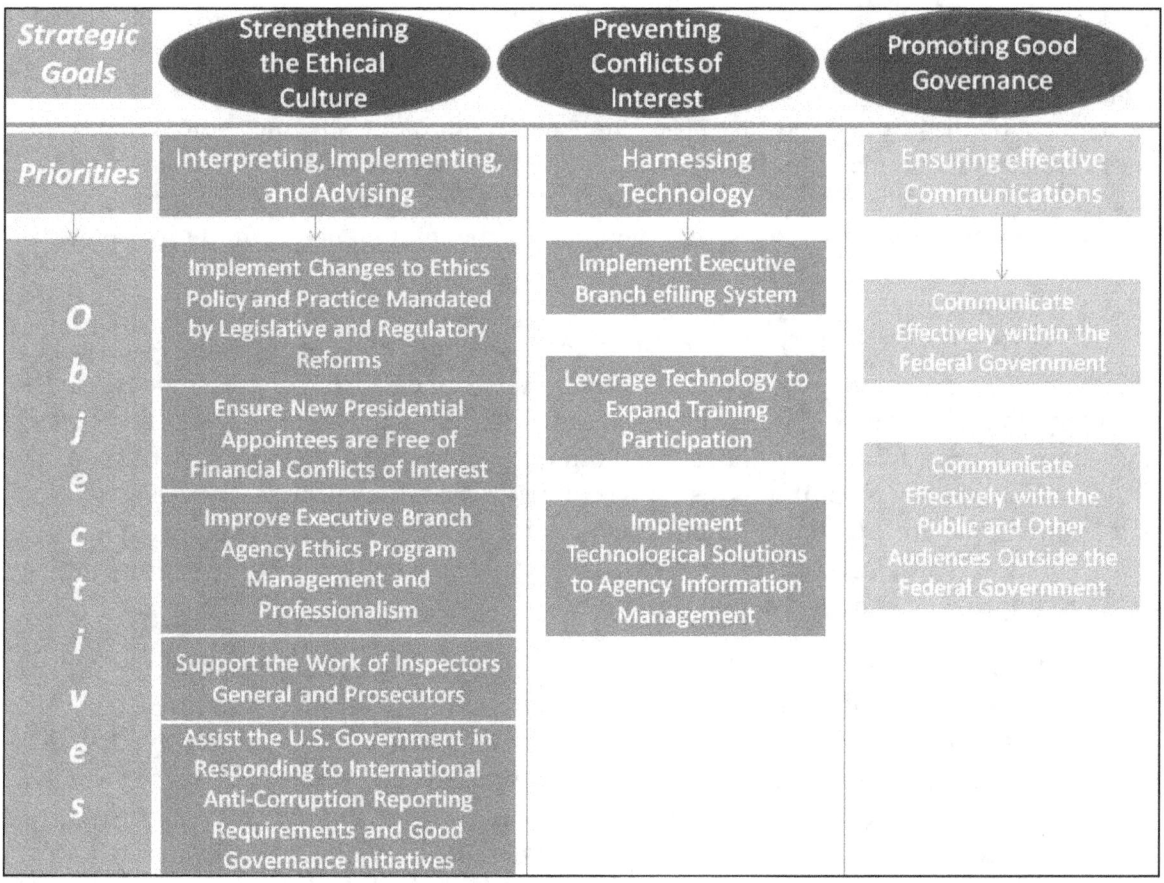

Figure 1

The following summary details the major accomplishments that OGE achieved in fiscal year 2013 in order to advance its priorities and to meet each of its objectives.

Priority 1: Interpreting, Implementing, and Advising on Government Ethics Laws, Policies, and Program Management

In fiscal year 2013, OGE undertook numerous efforts and initiatives to advance its priority of interpreting, implementing, and advising on ethics laws, policies, and program management. Notably, OGE implemented several changes in the executive branch ethics program that were necessitated by legislative or regulatory reforms. During this period, OGE also continued to ensure that new Presidential appointees were free of financial conflicts of interest and took steps to improve overall ethics program management and professionalism. Finally, OGE provided support and assistance to the work of inspectors general and to international anti-corruption and good governance initiatives.

The most far-reaching and complex changes to the executive branch ethics program in fiscal year 2013 were the result of the passage of the Stop Trading on Congressional Knowledge Act of 2012 (STOCK Act). To assist agencies in effectively implementing the STOCK Act, OGE issued several pieces of legal guidance outlining the new financial disclosure reporting procedures and requirements for periodic transaction reporting, as well as the employment negotiation notification and recusal requirements. OGE also provided training to hundreds of executive branch agency ethics officials, as well as administrative law judges, and members of the intelligence community on the various provisions of the STOCK Act.

In fiscal year 2013, OGE also published a legislative Legal Advisory analyzing the significant ethics-related legislative activity during the 112th Congress, including key statutory changes including the STOCK Act. In addition to the STOCK Act, the Legal Advisory addressed the Presidential Appointment Efficiency and Streamlining Act of 2011, which, among other things, established the President's working group on streamlining the Presidential appointments process. OGE's Director participated in the working group, which issued two reports to Congress in fiscal year 2013 recommending ways to improve the appointment process.

Another change that resulted in far-reaching ethics implications in fiscal year 2013 was the decision in *United States v. Windsor* case in which the Supreme Court found Section 3 of the Defense of Marriage Act to be unconstitutional. Shortly after this decision, OGE issued a Legal Advisory providing guidance on the effect of the Supreme Court's decision on the Federal ethics provisions that use the terms "spouse," "marriage," and "relative." As a result of the decision, and after a comprehensive consultative process between OGE and the Department of Justice, OGE issued a Legal Advisory explaining that Federal ethics rules and requirements now apply to employees in same-sex marriages in the same way that they apply to opposite-sex marriages. In addition to the Legal advisory, OGE provided language approved by the Department of Justice that agency ethics officials could use to proactively notify all agency employees of the new requirements.

In order to alert and assist agency ethics officials regarding other new or emerging issues and to ensure the uniform application of laws within the executive branch ethics program, OGE also provided legal guidance concerning ethics implications of certain appropriations act provisions. For instance, OGE issued guidance summarizing the new high-dollar value conference reporting requirements under the Consolidated and Further Continuing Appropriations Act of 2013. Further, OGE issued guidance reminding ethics officials and employees that ethics laws and rules apply to Federal employees who are in a furlough status as a result of sequestration.

In addition to issuing formal guidance, OGE routinely provided advice and assistance in response to requests from a variety of stakeholders. Notably, OGE responded to over 85 requests for technical assistance from the Congress on issues including the STOCK Act and its amendments, financial disclosure and the Presidential nomination process, post-government employment, gifts, and outside positions. The provision of this type of assistance helped to build understanding of the executive branch ethics program among congressional staff and to inform potential statutory revisions to ethics laws.

On the regulatory front, OGE published a final rule amending the regulation that describes financial interests that are exempt from the prohibition on employees participating in their official capacities in particular matters in which they have personal financial interests. These final rule amendments: (1) created a new exemption permitting a government employee to participate in a particular matter affecting the financial interests of a nonprofit organization in which the employee serves in an official capacity as officer, director, or trustee; and (2) revised the existing exemption for interests in the holdings of sector mutual funds to clarify that the exemption applies to interests in the holdings of sector unit investment trusts. The former exemption will, among other things, contribute significantly to the accomplishment of the statutory mission of agencies and will facilitate the professional development of government scientists and engineers.

OGE also jointly issued two new supplemental agency ethics regulations with financial regulatory agencies. These regulations more closely align the ability of the agencies' employees to own certain financial assets and participate in outside activities related to the missions of the agencies.

Strategic Objective: Ensure New Presidential Appointees are Free of Financial Conflicts of Interest

OGE reviews the financial interests of Presidentially-appointed, Senate-confirmed nominees for possible conflicts of interest with their prospective duties. As a result of the 2012 Presidential election, in fiscal year 2013 OGE reviewed 68 percent more PAS nominee public financial disclosure reports than it reviewed in fiscal year 2012. OGE prioritized its responsibility for reviewing and certifying PAS nominee financial disclosure reports and shifted its staff resources to timely review the significantly increased volume of reports. This cyclical increase in volume, owing to the transition from the first term to the second term of the Administration, necessitated that OGE train additional internal staff to meet increased demand. Targeted staff underwent intensive financial disclosure review training which included instructor-led courses, practical exercises using complex hypothetical reports, one-on-one mentoring by experienced reviewers, and supplemental instructional forums. In fiscal year 2013, OGE reviewed the reports of nominees for approximately 28 percent of the roughly 1,100 Senate-confirmed, Presidential appointees. By leveraging existing resources, OGE was able to meet the priorities set by the White House and the Senate.

OGE also identifies and resolves potential conflicts of interest on the part of the nominees by establishing written ethics agreements with them prior to their confirmations. OGE monitored the timeliness of compliance with these ethics agreements through the collection and review of documentation received by agency ethics officials. Forty-five PAS appointees entered into ethics agreements that required compliance documentation in fiscal year 2013. Agency ethics officials reported that 96 percent of these individuals complied with their ethics agreements within the established timeframes.

To ensure that executive branch leaders who have been appointed by the President and confirmed by the Senate remain free of conflicts of interest after taking office, OGE reviews their annual and termination public financial disclosure reports. OGE took significant steps in fiscal year 2013 to improve the efficiency and effectiveness of this review process. As a result of these improvements, OGE completed its review of 1,383 new entrant, annual, and termination public financial disclosure reports required to be submitted to OGE in fiscal year 2013. Additionally, OGE reviewed 392 periodic transaction reports in fiscal year 2013, the first year in which such reports were required as a result of the STOCK Act.

One of OGE's new Director's first initiatives and OGE's most notable accomplishments in fiscal year 2013 was improving the security, accountability, and integrity of its financial disclosure program. Through the extraordinary efforts of several cross-agency teams OGE closed out a significant backlog of PAS annual and termination public financial disclosure reports. First, OGE staff reviewed all PAS public financial disclosure reports that were pending OGE certification. Within the 60-day deadline established by the Director, staff working in an office-wide effort identified and completed reviews of 170 reports, representing a 4-year backlog. As a second step in this effort, OGE staff physically audited and examined the complete inventory of 4,296 report files. This inventory was the first, and perhaps the most significant, step toward completely reconciling the physical file inventory with the virtual records inventory of financial disclosure reports in OGE's history. As a third step, OGE staff enhanced the procedures for maintaining and tracking the reports that come to OGE for final review, including centralizing the physical filing and location of the report files.

To further ensure that PAS officials are free of conflicts of interest, in fiscal year 2013, OGE issued its fourth annual report on compliance with and implementation of the President's Executive Order on Ethics (Executive Order 13490). OGE found that during calendar year 2012, agencies successfully administered the Ethics Pledge required by the Executive Order. Of significance, 618 of 619 appointees required to sign the Ethics Pledge in 2012 had done so. One appointee resigned prior to signing the Ethics Pledge, but would have been required to sign it if the appointee had remained in the position.

Strategic Objective: Improve Executive Branch Agency Ethics Program Management and Professionalism

In fiscal year 2013, OGE improved executive branch ethics program management and professionalism by augmenting its ethics program review process, refining program management metrics, expanding educational offerings for ethics officials, and formalizing its commitment to the continuous professional development of its staff.

On-site reviews of agency ethics programs continued to be an important component of OGE's statutorily mandated oversight activities in fiscal year 2013. The primary objective of reviews is to report on the strengths and vulnerabilities of the program by evaluating agency compliance with ethics requirements, and ethics-related systems, processes, and procedures. OGE also identifies and shares model practices as part of its strategy for improving agency ethics programs. In the third quarter of fiscal year 2013, OGE developed a new inspection review methodology to augment its review program. The objective of an inspection is to provide a useful snapshot of the quality of agency implementation of selected core ethics program elements. Inspections will allow OGE to more efficiently exercise oversight and ensure on-site monitoring of a significantly greater number of agency programs than would be possible exclusively through plenary reviews.

Notable among OGE's review achievements in fiscal year 2013 was the follow-up work OGE conducted related to its 2012 Post-Election Readiness review. OGE worked with agencies to address vulnerabilities identified during the review that could impair the ability of agency ethics officials to conduct timely, accurate, and consistent conflict of interest reviews of PAS nominee financial disclosure reports. As a direct result of the Post-Election Readiness review and follow-up work, the Inspector General for an agency undertook a special review of the agency's ethics program due to significant concerns highlighted in OGE's review report.

Also of note, in March 2013, the National Academy of Public Administration (NAPA) emphasized the value of OGE's program review function in its independent, congressionally mandated report on the STOCK Act. NAPA noted that program reviews are a substantial reason for the effective government-wide ethics program. It also stated that OGE's follow-up reviews have successfully underscored the need to find solutions and held agencies accountable for making needed changes. In an effort to continue to improve the efficiency and effectiveness of OGE's reviews and the review selection process, OGE also standardized its review activities in fiscal year 2013 by developing new standard operating procedures.

In fiscal year 2013, OGE further advanced its priority of improving agency ethics program management and professionalism by significantly expanding educational offerings for ethics officials. For example, OGE delivered 27 instructor-led classroom and web-based training courses to approximately 1,762 ethics officials on a variety of topics. OGE also provided ethics presentations and instruction in various other formats reaching 4,249 ethics officials and other government employees. Finally, in, August of 2013, OGE partnered with the U.S. Department of Agriculture to offer the first Government Ethics Symposium. During this single-day event, OGE trained more than 200 ethics officials from more than 40 departments and agencies on the ethics rules surrounding the lifecycle of a Presidential appointee, model ethics program management practices, and the implications for the ethics rules after the Supreme Court's decision in *Windsor v. United States*. OGE plans to build upon the success of this event by partnering with other departments and agencies to host twice annual Government Ethics Symposia.

OGE also took steps to enhance program management and professionalism in fiscal year 2013 by offering additional educational opportunities to the geographically dispersed community of ethics officials in an efficient and fiscally responsible manner. For example, OGE developed and delivered 14 virtual distance learning events. These training events covered topics such as STOCK Act requirements, OGE's recently issued regulatory exemption to 18 U.S.C. § 208 for service on outside boards in an official capacity, and navigation of the agency supplemental standards of conduct regulation process. Live presentations of these events reached 2,487 officials and recordings of the presentations were accessed by an additional 1,400 distinct users.

A vital component of ensuring successful program management is an effective succession plan. To assist agencies with succession planning in their ethics programs, OGE developed, during fiscal year 2013, the Instructor Development Program (IDP), a certificate program for ethics instructors who, upon successful completion, will be qualified to effectively deliver OGE-developed ethics courses in their own agencies and throughout the executive branch. This qualification will assist them in ascending to higher positions within their programs as senior program leaders depart or retire.

Finally, in order to assist executive branch ethics officials in the effective management of their ethics programs, OGE requires a staff with state-of-the-art ethics knowledge, skills, and abilities. To ensure the continuing excellence of OGE's personnel, OGE launched an employee development program in fiscal year 2013 to provide time, resources, and support for the continuing professional development of OGE staff. The program commits up to 10 percent of a participating employee's duty time to professional development activities such as engaging in research, attending internal training, and participating in mentoring and coaching activities. The program is cost-effective because it uses internal resources, results in the development of products that can be re-used, contributes to knowledge sharing, and plans for succession at a time when government is facing an increase in retirements among its employees.

Strategic Objective: Support the Work of Inspectors General and Prosecutors

In fiscal year 2013, OGE provided direct support to inspector general (IG) investigators and Federal prosecutors on the interpretation and application of the conflict of interest laws and ethics rules. OGE also collaborated more generally with these groups in order to share ethics related information of mutual interest.

In particular, OGE continued to collaborate with the IG community through the Council of Inspectors General on Integrity and Efficiency (CIGIE) and the IG Academy, as well as with prosecutors. OGE leadership actively participated as a member of CIGIE, which examines allegations of misconduct against IGs and their direct reports. The goal of these interactions is to assist IGs and prosecutors in understanding the complexities of the ethics laws and regulations as they relate to ethics-related investigations and how effective ethics programs support enforcement.

Additionally, OGE continued to provide training support to IGs. Notably, OGE provided its core curriculum on conflicts of interest to members of the Council of Counsels to Inspectors General. OGE instructors also provided training at the IG Academy. This training on investigating ethics-related matters and working with ethics officials has become a standard part of the IG Academy's curriculum, and complements a web-based training module that OGE developed for IG investigators.

Finally, at the request of the IG Academy, OGE staff participated in the Public Corruption Investigations Training Program Curriculum Review Conference. OGE's participation in the conference led to several modifications to the training program, including increased training on public corruption statutes and increased class time devoted to practical skills training for investigators.

Strategic Objective: Assist the United States Government in Responding to International Anti- Corruption Reporting Requirements and Good Governance Initiatives

Through a variety of multilateral and bilateral activities and at the request of the Department of State, OGE continued to support U.S. government anti-corruption reporting requirements and good governance goals in fiscal year 2013. Of note, OGE provided substantial support for U.S. participation in anti-corruption mutual evaluation mechanisms designed to monitor compliance with international anti-corruption standards. OGE served as primary lead in researching and writing the U.S. response to questionnaires and responding to other calls for information related to good governance. OGE also supported U.S. participation, through the provision of technical assistance to or service on, U.S. delegations in other multilateral groups and programs. Finally, OGE officials served as subject matter expert panelists in several international seminars and workshops.

Priority 2: Harnessing Technology to Promote Transparency, Education, and Oversight

In fiscal year 2013, OGE continued to leverage technology in order to promote transparency in the executive branch ethics program, to provide training and educational materials, and to enhance its oversight function.

Strategic Objective: Implement Executive Branch-Wide Electronic Filing of Public Financial Disclosure Reports

In fiscal year 2013, OGE received funding for and began the development of the electronic Federal Ethics and Disclosure System (eFEDS), the electronic filing system for executive branch public financial disclosure report filers mandated by the STOCK Act. When completed, this system will greatly enhance the filing, review, and program management aspects of the executive branch public financial disclosure program. It will also increase OGE's oversight capability by allowing OGE to monitor agencies' progress in administering their individual financial disclosure programs in real time and to generate reports identifying trends and weaknesses in their programs.

A cross-divisional OGE team of attorneys and analysts developed the content for eFEDS, which will lead filers through a serious of questions, the answers to which will populate the required fields of the public financial disclosure report. This question and answer format will simplify the reporting process and will greatly improve the accuracy of the reported information. The improved accuracy of reporting will in turn enhance ethics officials' ability to identify and resolve conflicts of interest.

To enhance filer experience, OGE also worked closely with a team of user experience professionals. The user experience team is responsible for ensuring that the user interface - i.e., what filers see in any given section of the system - is clear, easily understood, and logically leads filers through the reporting process.

Throughout the system development process beginning in the fourth quarter of fiscal year 2013, OGE has collaborated extensively with financial disclosure report filers, executive branch agency ethics officials, and ethics officials and system developers from the other branches of government, to share ideas and to ensure that eFEDS meets the needs of all stakeholders. This collaboration included dozens of meetings and information-sharing events, as well as OGE's administration of an electronic survey of public filers, which was used to gather feedback about their needs and expectations. OGE also created an online forum to provide updates to ethics officials and to collect input from the ethics community regarding the development of the system.

Strategic Objective: Leverage Technology to Expand Training Participation

OGE also continued to explore ways to use technology to provide timely information to executive branch ethics officials, the vast majority of whom are located outside the Washington, DC area. One of OGE's major accomplishments in this area during fiscal year 2013 was the creation of the Institute for Ethics in Government (IEG). IEG is a virtual "ethics university" on the MAX.gov website, a government-wide collaboration, data collection, and information sharing site. All Federal government employees in the executive branch are eligible to register for a MAX Account. Government employees with a MAX Account can view the course offerings and register or apply to participate. Individuals can also access all the materials and recordings for OGE's monthly webinar series on-demand, and can browse and download the education and job-related products in the IEG Store. The IEG site also allows ethics officials to share their own products with the ethics community.

OGE further leveraged technology in fiscal year 2013 by launching an official agency Twitter account to increase visibility of the executive branch ethics program and provide accurate executive branch ethics information to the public and media, thereby promoting public confidence. Using its Twitter account, OGE directs its external stakeholders to detailed information on its website and provides its external audiences an additional way to stay current with OGE's latest publications as well as changes in executive branch ethics laws, regulations, and programs.

Strategic Objective: Implement Technological Solutions to Agency Information Management

OGE also implemented new technical solutions for managing and measuring performance in fiscal year 2013. Most notably, OGE developed and launched two new electronic information management systems, the Agency Information Management System (AIMS) and the Financial Disclosure Tracking System (FDTS).

AIMS tracks and manages OGE interactions, such as incoming requests for guidance and interpretation from over 130 executive branch agencies, Congress, the media, and the public. The system also provides OGE officials instant access to ethics program-related information about all executive branch agencies.

FDTS tracks the collection, review, and final action on financial disclosure reports, ethics agreements, certificates of divestiture, and trust documents for Presidential nominees, appointees, and Designated Agency Ethics Officials (DAEOs). This web-based system provides OGE the ability to follow the progress of financial disclosure-related work throughout the agency and to promptly determine the status of financial disclosure reports.

Priority 3: Ensuring Effective Communications to Enhance Understanding of Government Ethics Laws, Policies, and Program Management, and to Promote Transparency, Education, and Oversight

OGE took undertook several initiatives in fiscal year 2013 to enhance its communications efforts. These initiatives were targeted at audiences both within and outside of the Federal government.

Strategic Objective: Communicate Effectively Within the Federal Government

To enhance communication within the Federal government, OGE convened numerous meetings and participated in various outreach efforts with a variety of audiences in fiscal year 2013. For example, OGE organized regular meetings with the most senior ethics practitioners from all three branches of the Federal government in order to discuss issues of common interest and to build a professional network dedicated to improving ethics government-wide. The relationships and lines of communication developed in these OGE-led meetings proved invaluable in reaching common understandings of ongoing and emerging issues, such as the STOCK Act. Additionally, the improved communications facilitated by these meetings contributed to a large increase in the number of requests from the legislative branch for technical assistance from OGE on a wide range of issues.

During fiscal year 2013, OGE also organized a large number of meetings, conference calls, and webinars with senior executive branch agency ethics officials. For instance, OGE held regular meetings with executive branch DAEOs. Through these meetings, OGE shared information relevant to managing an effective ethics program, discussed current ethics issues facing the executive branch, and received agency input.

In addition, OGE used the MAX.gov platform to provide information to and collaborate with ethics officials. Specifically, in fiscal year 2013, OGE developed the Agency Assistance and Outreach Forum on MAX.gov to engage ethics officials in an informal exchange of information about a variety of government ethics topics. The forum provides up-to-date news on OGE's latest advisories, programs, and educational opportunities; shares ethics-related news articles; and relays information on ethics-related legislation that OGE is monitoring.

To further its communication efforts, OGE launched two distance-learning series through low cost teleconferences: the Ethics Fundamentals Series and the Advanced Practitioner Series. The Ethics Fundamentals Series addresses the basics of government ethics in a format convenient to part-time ethics officials and ethics officials in the field. The Advanced Practitioner Series addresses advanced topics in a format that is tailored to experienced ethics practitioners and provides a forum for these officials to share their experiences and expertise with one another. In fiscal year 2013, OGE hosted six Fundamentals Series events and eight Advanced Practitioner events.

Additionally, OGE utilized a teleconference format to host five separate workshops covering public financial disclosure and outside activities regulations. These teleconferences allowed OGE to reach a large number of ethics officials at minimal cost. Further, OGE received positive feedback from participants regarding the quality of the material presented during these teleconferences.

OGE continued to provide support to agency ethics officials through its Desk Officer program. Desk Officers provide instant access to expert advice in applying the ethics laws and regulations. During fiscal year 2013, OGE Desk Officers responded to approximately 1,927 requests for guidance. In response to the Annual Survey of Ethics Officials, a majority of ethics officials responded positively when asked if OGE Desk Officers support helps them perform their job.

OGE also focused on effective communication and collaboration with specific Federal groups, such as Federal advisory committee members, senior managers, and administrative law judges. Through these interactions, OGE highlighted ethics issues specific to these and other groups, and alerted them to any new ethics laws, regulations, policies, or guidance. For example, OGE attended and contributed to the 58th Plenary Session of the Administrative Conference of the United States concerning adopting recommendations to improve consistency in social security disability adjudication and improving administrative rulemaking procedures. OGE also presented on various topics at the Interagency Ethics Council, including providing an overview of model practices concerning the review of PAS public financial disclosure reports.

Finally, OGE contributed its expertise and significant support to other Federal agency training programs in fiscal year 2013. For example, OGE participated in OPM's Employee and Labor Relations Roundtable by providing attendees an introduction to the executive branch ethics program with a focus on helping human resource professionals understand the ethics rules and manage risk. OPM broadcasted the event across the nation to 550 sites, many of which had multiple attendees. In addition, OGE provided ethics training at the General Services Administration's Federal Advisory Committee Act management training course and at the Government Accountability Office's annual Appropriations Forum on "Public Private Partnerships." OGE also delivered presentations on the Procurement Integrity Act and organizational risk identification and mitigation at the 2013 Deputy Ethics Counselor Workshop at the Department of Health and Human Services. Notably, in April of 2013, OGE provided training at the request of the White House on public financial disclosure. The training introduced attendees to the critical conflicts of interest and financial disclosure concepts.

In fiscal year 2013, OGE substantially increased its efforts to reach audiences outside of the Federal government, including members of the general public, state and local governments, private sector organizations, professional associations, government watchdog groups, the media, and foreign delegations.

As part of the agency's continuing effort to promote transparency and accountability, and thereby promote public confidence in government, OGE continued to make public records readily available on the OGE website. Specifically, in fiscal year 2013, OGE posted 1,013 public financial disclosure reports and 505 semiannual agency reports of travel payments accepted from non-Federal sources.

In addition to proactively sharing information through mechanisms such as its website, OGE routinely responded to requests from private sector and other non-government organizations asking for assistance in clarifying the application of Federal ethics laws and rules to their current employees, or Federal employees who volunteer at their organizations. By sharing its expertise with these entities, OGE helps to ensure that neither they nor their employees inadvertently violate Federal ethics rules. For example, in fiscal year 2013 OGE directly issued advice to the counsel of a university on the application of an exemption to the post-employment criminal conflict of interest statute and to a publishing company concerning the use of title creating the appearance of governmental sanction. In both instances, OGE clarified the application of these laws as they applied to former or current government employees associated with each entity.

OGE continued its involvement with private sector and professional organizations that focus on ethics, such as the Ethics Resource Center, the Ethics and Compliance Officer Association, and the Council for Governmental Ethics Laws. OGE's involvement with these organizations not only fosters communications for its own sake, but also leads to innovations in OGE's practices related to training, program management, and performance evaluation.

OGE also engaged with good governance and watchdog groups in fiscal year 2013. This direct, proactive communication ensures that these non-Federal organizations and, by extension, the general public, understand the executive branch ethics program and the reasoning behind various policy decisions. These efforts also help OGE to be transparent and responsive to public concerns.

Some examples of OGE's collaboration with non-Federal organizations in fiscal year 2013 include OGE's participation in several programs with representatives from the American Bar Association Public Contract Law Section's Ethics, Compliance, and Professional Responsibility Committee; The Partnership for Public Service; and the ABA Criminal Justice Section as well as presentations at the First Amendment Center; and the "Disclosure about Who is Influencing Politics and Policy" symposium hosted by an organization named OpentheGovernment.org.

OGE continued to share its legal analysis, programmatic experience, and model practices with state and local government agencies involved in administering programs that support good governance. Much of that sharing occurred through or because of OGE's active participation with the Council on Governmental Ethics Laws (COGEL), an organization of Federal, state, and local government agencies whose responsibilities include ethics, campaign finance, freedom of information, and lobbying disclosure. OGE exchanged good practices through presentations at COGEL's annual conference, posted on the COGEL website, and responded to direct requests for information from state and local jurisdictions.

Finally, OGE continued to meet with foreign public and private sector groups traveling under the auspices of the State Department International Visitor Leadership Program and other similar programs. These delegations come to OGE to learn about the ethics program in the executive branch and how that program fits under the broader rubric of good governance and transparency. In fiscal year 2013, OGE briefed 35 foreign delegations comprised of 494 individuals representing 65 countries. In addition, at a program hosted by Georgetown University, OGE addressed a class of graduate students from Salzburg University who were completing studies in public administration on ethics and organizational risk management.

Creating and Promoting a Positive Performance Culture

In addition to advancing the three priorities discussed above, OGE's new Director emphasized the role of internal communications in promoting a culture of performance during fiscal year 2013. As a result, OGE enhanced internal communications through a variety of methods such as:

- Conducting quarterly "all hands" meetings with the entire OGE staff to report progress toward goals and to provide clear and direct communication about OGE's priorities and direction;

- Holding regular Executive and Senior Staff meetings to discuss agency goals, priorities, and the status of significant program activities; and

- Holding supervisors accountable for ensuring ongoing communication regarding OGE goals and priorities with all staff.

In addition to emphasizing internal communications, OGE took several other steps during fiscal year 2013 to promote a culture of performance, including:

- Preparing a new strategic plan covering fiscal years 2014 through 2017, with input from stakeholders in the executive branch ethics community, Congress, good government groups, and the general public;

- Supporting a variety of flexible work and telework schedules consistent with OGE's team-oriented environment;

- Continuing support for the agency's Equal Employment Opportunity (EEO) and Diversity and Inclusion programs; and

- Encouraging employees to participate voluntarily in direct and consequential community service consistent with applicable Executive Orders and Office of Personnel Management guidelines.

Conclusion

In conclusion, the performance highlights described in Part II reflect a cross-functional staff dedicated to advancing the mission of OGE by using innovative, cost-effective, and collaborative solutions.

Part III – Management Discussion & Analysis of Results

This section provides data on OGE's success in achieving its strategic objectives and performance measures during fiscal year 2013. The following measurements are based on statistical data from a variety of existing sources, including post-training evaluations; an annual ethics program questionnaire, surveys following program reviews, and the Annual Survey of Ethics Officials.[1]

Strategic Goal 1 – Strengthening Ethical Culture within the Executive Branch

Objective 1.1: Improve the Effectiveness of Ethics Policy

OGE continues to earn high marks from ethics officials for providing guidance to improve the effectiveness of ethics policy. OGE's survey of agency ethics officials' customer satisfaction focused on three areas: (1) the usefulness of OGE guidance; (2) the effectiveness of OGE guidance; and (3) OGE's responsiveness to emerging ethics program issues.

The results related to Objective 1.1 performance measures show that OGE exceeded each of its targets. (*See Figures 2, 3, and 4*)

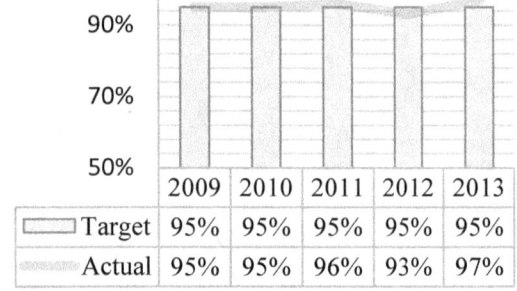

% of ethics officials who rate OGE guidance as useful

	2009	2010	2011	2012	2013
Target	95%	95%	95%	95%	95%
Actual	95%	95%	96%	93%	97%

Figure 3

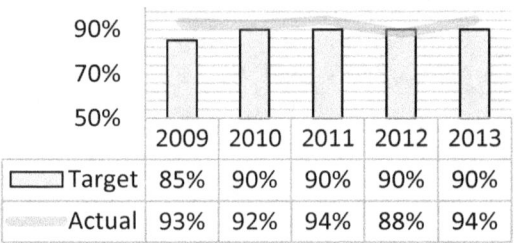

% of ethics officials who say OGE provides the guidance needed to perform their ethics duties effectively

	2009	2010	2011	2012	2013
Target	85%	90%	90%	90%	90%
Actual	93%	92%	94%	88%	94%

Figure 2

% of ethics officials who rate OGE as responsive to emerging ethics program issues

	2009	2010	2011	2012	2013
Target	80%	80%	85%	85%	85%
Actual	88%	87%	90%	85%	87%

Figure 4

[1] Several of these performance measures are based on data collected from the Annual Survey of Ethics Officials. The survey is distributed to Designated Agency Ethics Officials, Alternate Designated Agency Ethics Officials and the Agency Ethics Points of Contact. The survey responses are anonymous and agencies may submit more than one response. The response rate for 2012 survey was 35% (n=112).

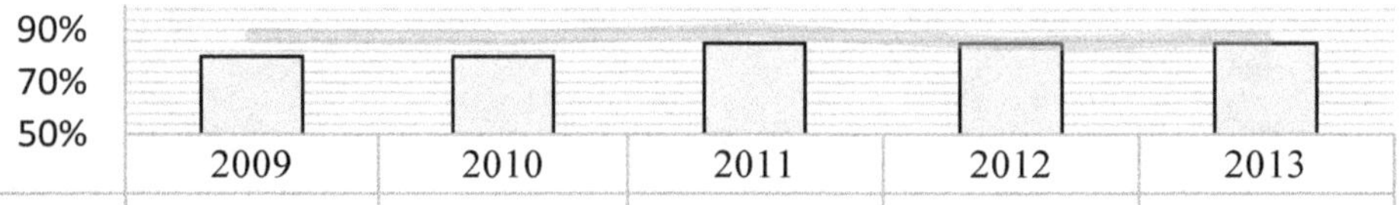

While OGE continually receives a great deal of information about ethics program administration, on-site monitoring is OGE's most effective tool for maintaining and improving the quality and consistency of the executive branch's ethics program. OGE's plenary reviews are designed to mitigate program vulnerabilities, disseminate model practices, and encourage ongoing dialogue among ethics officials and with OGE Desk Officers. In fiscal year 2013, OGE completed plenary reviews and follow-up monitoring for more than 35 executive branch agencies. Figure 5 shows that OGE exceeded its target to add value to agency ethics program and to share model practices during the program review process.

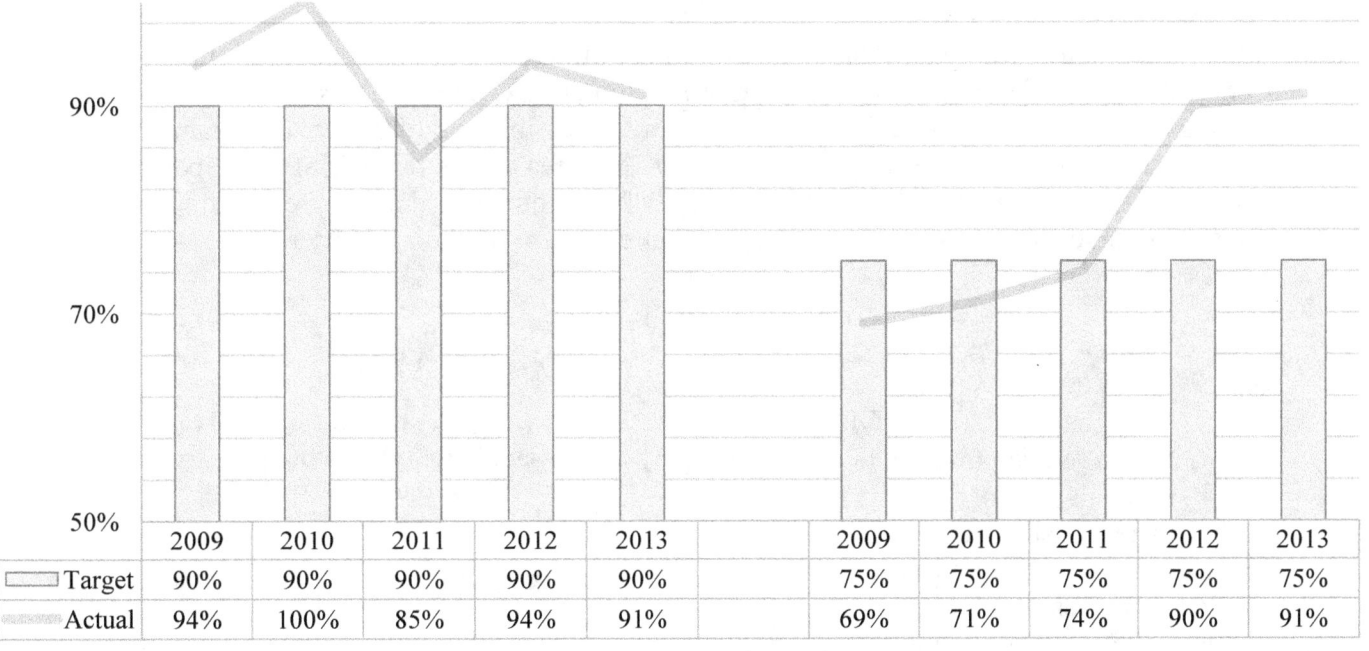

	% of ethics officials who view OGE's program review process as adding value to their own						% of ethics officials who are satisfied with information shared on ethics program model practices				
	2009	2010	2011	2012	2013		2009	2010	2011	2012	2013
Target	90%	90%	90%	90%	90%		75%	75%	75%	75%	75%
Actual	94%	100%	85%	94%	91%		69%	71%	74%	90%	91%

Figure 5

17

While OGE continued to provide support to ethics officials through education and training opportunities, OGE missed its satisfaction target based on results from the Annual Survey of Ethics Officials (*Figure 6*). OGE believes this decline may be linked to OGE's reredeployment of a revamped education and training program that focused on expanding access to ethics officials across the executive branch using new methods of delivery. (*See pages 9, 10, 12, 13, and 14 for additional information about OGE's education and training program*). OGE believes this number will

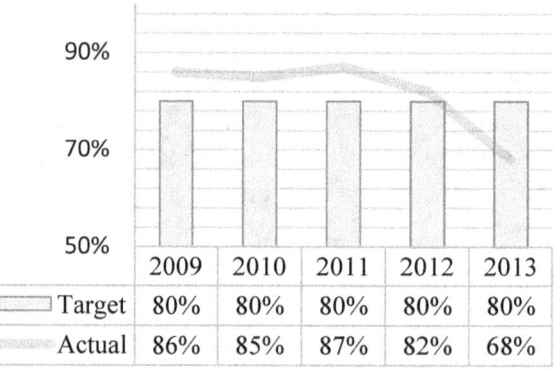

% of ethics officials who are satisfied with education and training provided to support ethics officials

	2009	2010	2011	2012	2013
Target	80%	80%	80%	80%	80%
Actual	86%	85%	87%	82%	68%

Figure 6

increase as ethics officials become more familiar with OGE's refocused education program and new training products. In addition, though OGE missed this target, other data sources indicate that OGE's training is more accessible and effective. For example, as a result of these new methods of delivery, OGE increased the number of participants' with access to live training by 254%. Further, 94% of course participants responding to post-training evaluations stated that they are better able to do their job after OGE training (*See Figure 7*).

Objective 1.3: Increase Employees' Awareness of Their Ethics Responsibilities

In fiscal year 2013, OGE continued to provide training to agency ethics officials to assist them in carrying out their responsibilities. Notably, 4,249 ethics officials registered for OGE training courses. As shown in Figure 7, ethics officials overwhelmingly reported that they are better able to do their jobs as a result of OGE training.

OGE missed targets regarding ethics officials satisfaction and incorporation of certain OGE training products (*Figures 8, 9, and 10*). In light of sequestration and a significant increase

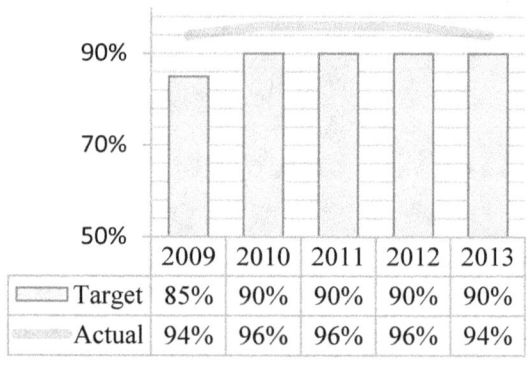

% of ethics officials reporting that they are better able to do their jobs as a result of OGE training

	2009	2010	2011	2012	2013
Target	85%	90%	90%	90%	90%
Actual	94%	96%	96%	96%	94%

Figure 7

(68%) in the workload of the nominee program, OGE shifted resources and de-emphasized its prior priority to create training products in fiscal year 2013. However, OGE still supported ethics officials through the creation of the IEG site which allows ethics officials to share their own training products with the ethics community. Since the site's creation, agencies have posted more than 20 training products. Moving forward, OGE will continue to encourage ethics officials to share their training products. In addition, OGE established new performance goals for fiscal year 2014 that align better with its revamped education and training program.

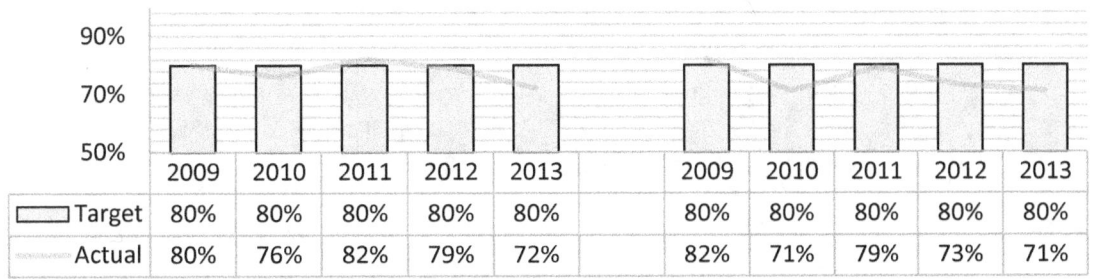

Figure 8

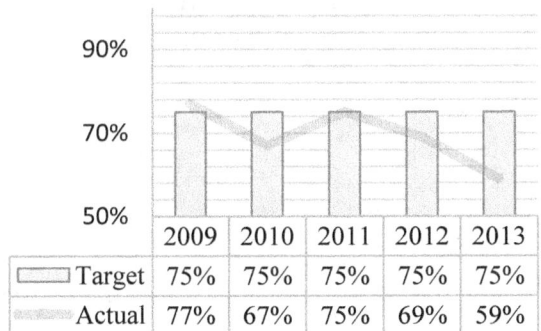

Figure 9

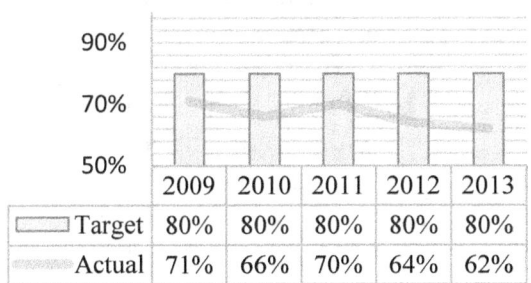

Figure 10

Objective 1.4: Increase OGE's Focus on Senior Officials' Roles in Implementing Ethics Programs

OGE recognizes and encourages senior officials to play a significant role in promoting an ethical culture and supporting the agency's ethics program. OGE's new Director is committed to continuing to promote leadership support of ethics programs. In fiscal year 2014, OGE will continue to leverage the program review and nominee process to highlight the importance of the executive branch ethics program and agency leadership's role in supporting it. Figures 11 and 12 show that OGE essentially met its targets for Strategic Objective 1.4.

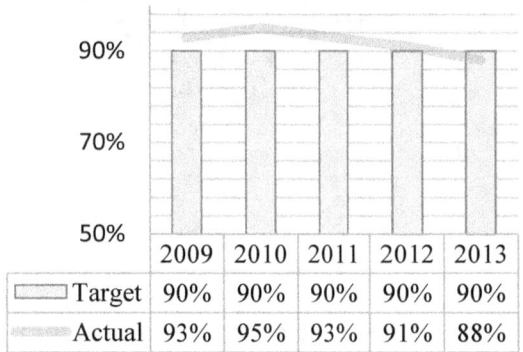

% of ethics officials who indicate that their agency's leaders pay attention to ethics

	2009	2010	2011	2012	2013
Target	90%	90%	90%	90%	90%
Actual	93%	95%	93%	91%	88%

Figure 11

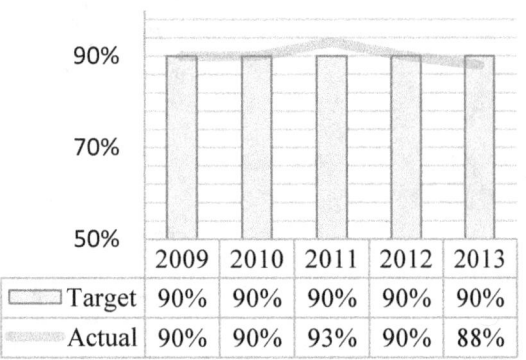

% of ethics officials who indicate that their agency's leaders demonstrate support for the ethics program

	2009	2010	2011	2012	2013
Target	90%	90%	90%	90%	90%
Actual	90%	90%	93%	90%	88%

Figure 12

Strategic Goal 2 – Preventing Conflicts of Interest

Objective 2.1: Enhance Assistance to the President and the Senate in the Presidential Appointment Process

In coordination with agency ethics officials, OGE monitors the timeliness of employee compliance with ethics agreements through documentation received by agency ethics officials. 45 PAS officials entered into ethics agreements that required compliance documentation in fiscal year 2013. As reported by DAEOs, 96 percent of ethics agreements were satisfied within statutory deadlines. (*See Figure 13*)

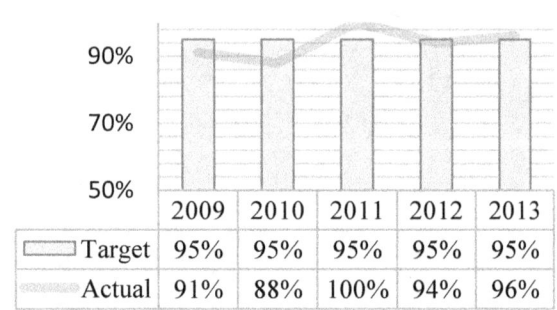

Compliance with ethics agreements within required timeframes

	2009	2010	2011	2012	2013
Target	95%	95%	95%	95%	95%
Actual	91%	88%	100%	94%	96%

Figure 13

Additionally, OGE measures the resolution of conflicts and technical reporting issues for nominee financial disclosure reports. OGE's established standard is to finalize conflict resolution and technical issues no later than 5 days after a nomination is made. OGE continues to demonstrate a high level of success in this area. (*See Figure 14*)

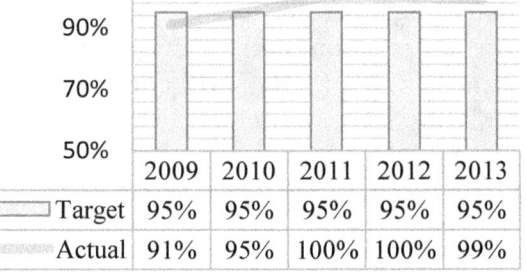

Resolution of conflicts and technical reporting issues for nominee financial disclosure reports no later than five days after a nomination is made

	2009	2010	2011	2012	2013
Target	95%	95%	95%	95%	95%
Actual	91%	95%	100%	100%	99%

Figure 14

Financial disclosure is the primary tool executive branch agencies use to identify and resolve potential conflicts of interest. Through monitoring and oversight, OGE ensures that agencies have implemented effective financial disclosure processes. Specifically, as part of the review process, OGE ensures that agencies provide public filers with feedback after reports have been reviewed and that agencies have written procedures for following up with delinquent filers. In fiscal year 2013, OGE exceeded its targets in this area. (*See Figure 15*)

% of agencies reviewed that provide public filers with feedback after reports have been reviewed   **% of agencies reviewed that have written procedures for following-up with delinquent filers**

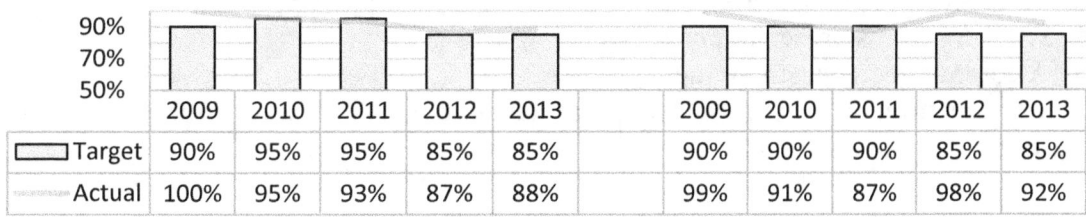

	2009	2010	2011	2012	2013		2009	2010	2011	2012	2013
Target	90%	95%	95%	85%	85%		90%	90%	90%	85%	85%
Actual	100%	95%	93%	87%	88%		99%	91%	87%	98%	92%

Figure 15

In furtherance of Objectives 2.2 and 2.3, OGE continued to encourage agencies to use alternative procedures for handling confidential financial disclosure in fiscal year 2013. Appropriate implementation of alternative procedures promotes efficient allocation of ethics program resources and allows agencies to focus resources on other important program objectives, including leadership support, succession planning, advice and counsel, and training. The figure to the right shows continued positive results. (*See Figure 16*)

Alternative forms judged by compliance division to be effectively managed

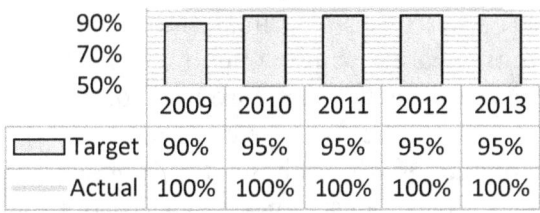

	2009	2010	2011	2012	2013
Target	90%	95%	95%	95%	95%
Actual	100%	100%	100%	100%	100%

Figure 16

Strategic Goal 3 – Promoting Good Governance

Objective 3.1: Increase OGE's Support of and Cooperation with Federal, State, and Local Agencies Implementing Programs that Help Support Good Governance

During fiscal year 2013, OGE actively coordinated and cooperated with other Federal, state, and local government agencies that have complementary missions and programs. During the fiscal year, OGE exceeded its target goals for programs and projects with other Federal, state, and local agencies both in terms of numbers and usefulness (*See Figure 17*). OGE evaluates the usefulness of its actions to others, by actual surveys or through written notes from those with whom OGE interacts. For some types of interactions, such as presentations to FACA committee managers or the IG Academy, recurrent requests for OGE's participation is an indication of the usefulness of the program to those audiences.

# of Outreach activities with Federal, state, and local entities

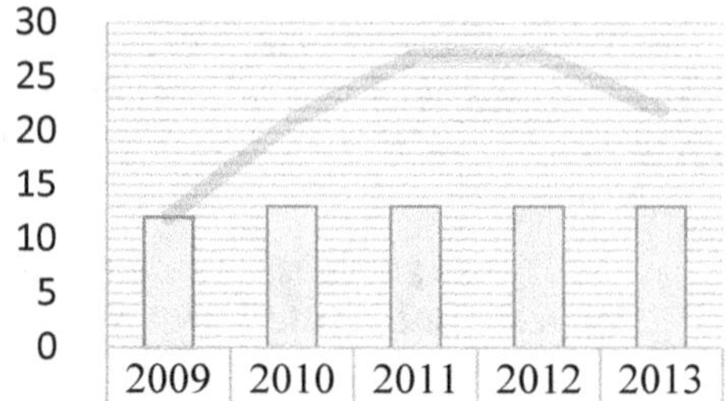

	2009	2010	2011	2012	2013
Target	12	13	13	13	13
Actual	12	21	27	27	22

Figure 17

Objective 3.2: Enhance Outreach to the Public, Private Sector, and Good Governance Groups

During fiscal year 2013, OGE exceeded its target to conduct outreach to the public, private sector, and good governance groups (*See Figure 18*). OGE's website is its primary tool for communicating with the public. OGE's website saw a 32% increase in unique visits during the fiscal year. In addition to conducting outreach, OGE responded to over 200 requests for assistance from these groups. Additional examples of specific outreach conducted by OGE to the public, private sector, and good governance groups are described in Part I. (*See information on pages 13-16*)

# of Outreach activities with public, private sector, and good governance groups

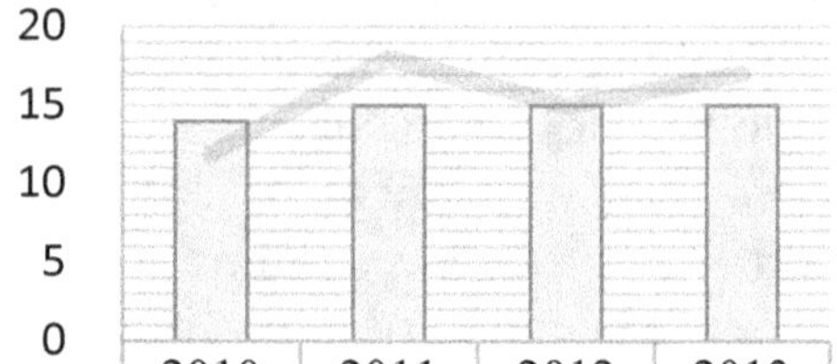

	2010	2011	2012	2013
Target	14	15	15	15
Actual	12	18	15	17

Figure 18

Objective 3.3 Support U.S. Foreign Policy Anti-Corruption and Good Governance Initiatives

In fiscal year 2013, OGE continued to receive and fulfill requests to participate in substantial programs and projects that help support U.S. foreign policy anti-corruption and good governance initiatives. Below is a list of some of the international organizations and programs with and in which OGE participated as expert evaluator in mutual evaluation mechanisms, as a subject-matter panelist, through provision of behind-the-scenes technical assistance, or through similar service:

- United Nations (UN): the UN Convention Against Corruption (UNCAC) Implementation Review Group and the UNCAC Working Group on Prevention;
- Council of Europe: the Group of States Against Corruption (GRECO);
- Asia-Pacific Economic Corporation (APEC): the Anti-Corruption and Transparency Working Group;
- Organization for Economic Co-operation and Development (OECD): the Public Governance Directorate Network on Public Sector Integrity; the Anti-Corruption Network for Eastern Europe; and
- Organization of American States (OAS): the follow-up mechanism of the Inter-American Convention Against Corruption (MESICIC).

Figure 19

OGE also continued to provide international technical assistance briefings to foreign officials from the public and private sector traveling under the auspices of the State Department International Visitor Leadership Program and other similar programs. This past fiscal year, 40 delegations comprised of 543 individuals representing 74 countries came to OGE to learn about the ethics program in the executive branch and how that program fits into the broader rubric of good governance principles.

In fiscal year 2013, OGE provided some form of technical assistance in support of U.S. foreign policy interests-- whether through international technical assistance briefings hosted domestically or through international presentations –to the countries highlighted in blue in figure 20.

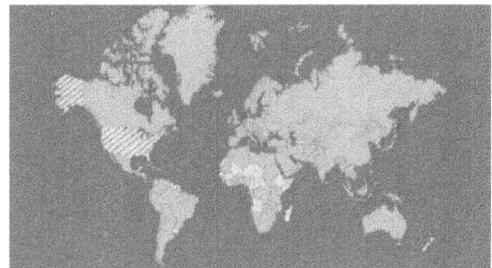

Figure 20

Annual Assurance Statement on Internal Controls and Internal Controls over Financial Reporting

OGE's management is responsible for establishing and maintaining effective internal control and financial management systems that meet the objectives of the Federal Managers' Financial Integrity Act (FMFIA). OGE conducted its assessment and compliance with applicable laws and regulations in accordance with OMB Circular A-123, Management's Responsibility for Internal Control. After a thorough review of the results, and to the best of my knowledge and belief, OGE can provide reasonable assurance that its internal control over the effectiveness and efficiency of operations and compliance with applicable laws and regulations as of September 30, 2013, was operating effectively and that no material weaknesses were found in the design or operations of the internal controls.

OGE relies on the U.S. Department of Treasury, Bureau of Fiscal Service (BFS), a shared service provider, for its accounting and financial reporting requirements. OGE obtains the Statement on Standards for Attestation Engagements No. 16 report from BFS, and reviews it to assist in assessing internal controls over OGE's financial reporting. After a thorough review of the results, OGE has not discovered any significant issues or deviations in its financial reporting during fiscal year 2013, and therefore concludes that OGE's internal controls over financial reporting are sufficiently strong.

OGE has no in-house financial systems. OGE has chosen to use Oracle Financials, hosted by BFS. Because of the rigorous testing that BFS undergoes, OGE considers this financial system to be reliable and effective.

Walter M. Shaub, Jr.
Director
U.S. Office of Government Ethics

Limitations of the Financial Statements

OGE's principal financial statements have been prepared to report its financial position and results of operations, pursuant to the requirements of 31 U.S.C. § 3515 (b). While the statements have been prepared from the books and records of OGE, in accordance with generally accepted accounting principles for Federal entities and the formats prescribed by OMB, the statements are in addition to the financial reports used to monitor and control budgetary resources, which are prepared from the same books and records. These statements should be read with the realization that they are for a component of the United States government, a sovereign entity.

INDEPENDENT AUDITOR'S REPORT

U.S. Office of Government Ethics
Washington, D.C.

Report on the Financial Statements

We have audited the accompanying balance sheets of the U.S. Office of Government Ethics (USOGE) as of September 30, 2013 and 2012, and the related statements of net cost, changes in net position, and budgetary resources, for the years then ended (collectively referred to as the financial statements), and the related notes to the financial statements.

Management's Responsibility for the Financial Statements

Management is responsible for the preparation and fair presentation of these financial statements in accordance with accounting principles generally accepted in the United States of America; this includes the design, implementation, and maintenance of internal control relevant to the preparation and fair presentation of financial statements that are free from material misstatement, whether due to fraud or error.

Auditor's Responsibility

Our responsibility is to express an opinion on these financial statements based on our audit. We conducted our audit in accordance with auditing standards generally accepted in the United States of America and the standards applicable to financial audits contained in *Government Auditing Standards*, issued by the Comptroller General of the United States; and the Office of Management and Budget (OMB) Bulletin No. 14-02, *Audit Requirements for Federal Financial Statements*, as amended. Those standards and OMB Bulletin No. 14-02, require that we plan and perform the audit to obtain reasonable assurance about whether the financial statements are free from material misstatements.

An audit involves performing procedures to obtain audit evidence about the amounts and disclosures in the financial statements. The procedures selected depend on the auditor's judgment, including the assessment of the risks of material misstatement of the financial statements, whether due to fraud or error. In making those risk assessments, the auditor considers internal control relevant to the entity's preparation and fair presentation of the financial statements in order to design audit procedures that are appropriate in the circumstances, but not for the purpose of expressing an opinion on the effectiveness of the entity's internal control. Accordingly, we express no such opinion. An audit also includes evaluating the appropriateness of accounting policies used and the reasonableness of significant accounting estimates made by management, as well as evaluating the overall presentation of the financial statements.

We believe that the audit evidence we have obtained is sufficient and appropriate to provide a basis for our audit opinion.

1101 MERCANTILE LANE, SUITE 122 • LARGO, MD 20774
PHONE: (240) 770-4900 • FAX: (301) 773-2090 • mail@brownco-cpas.com • www.brownco-cpas.com

26

Opinion on the Financial Statements

In our opinion, the financial statements referred to above present fairly, in all material respects, the financial position of the USOGE as of September 30, 2013 and 2012, and its net costs, changes in net position, and budgetary resources for the years then ended, in accordance with accounting principles generally accepted in the United States of America.

Other Matters

Accounting principles generally accepted in the United States of America require that the information in the Management's Discussion and Analysis (MD&A) and Required Supplementary Information (RSI) sections be presented to supplement the basic financial statements. Such information, although not a part of the basic financial statements, is required by the Federal Accounting Standards Advisory Board, who considers it to be an essential part of financial reporting for placing the basic financial statements in an appropriate operational, economic, or historical context. We have applied certain limited procedures to the required supplementary information in accordance with auditing standards generally accepted in the United States of America, which consisted of inquiries of management about the methods of preparing the information and comparing the information for consistency with management's responses to our inquiries, the basic financial statements, and other knowledge we obtained during our audit of the basic financial statements. We do not express an opinion or provide any assurance on the information because the limited procedures do not provide us with sufficient evidence to express an opinion or provide any assurance.

Report on Internal Control Over Financial Reporting

In planning and performing our audit of the financial statements, we considered the USOGE's internal control over financial reporting (internal control) to design audit procedures that are appropriate in the circumstances for the purpose of expressing an opinion on the financial statements, but not for the purpose of expressing an opinion on the effectiveness of USOGE's internal control. Accordingly, we do not express an opinion on the effectiveness of USOGE's internal control.

A *deficiency in internal control* exists when the design or operation of a control does not allow management or employees, in the normal course of performing their assigned functions, to prevent, or detect and correct, misstatements on a timely basis. A *material weakness* is a deficiency, or combination of deficiencies, in internal control, such that there is a reasonable possibility that a material misstatement of the entity's financial statements will not be prevented, or detected and corrected on a timely basis. A *significant deficiency* is a deficiency, or a combination of deficiencies, in internal control that is less severe than a material weakness, yet important enough to merit attention by those charged with governance.

Our consideration of the internal control was for the limited purpose described in the first paragraph of this section and was not designed to identify all deficiencies in internal control over financial reporting that might be deficiencies, significant deficiencies or material weaknesses. In our fiscal year 2013 audit, we did not identify any deficiencies in internal control that we consider to be a material weakness. However, material weaknesses may exist that have not been identified.

Report on Compliance and Other Matters

As part of obtaining reasonable assurance about whether USOGE's financial statements are free from material misstatement, we performed tests of its compliance with applicable provisions of laws, regulations, contracts and grant agreements, noncompliance with which could have a direct and material effect on the determination of financial statement amounts. However, providing an opinion on compliance with those provisions was not an objective of our audit, and accordingly, we do not express such an opinion. The results of our tests disclosed no instances of noncompliance or other matters that are required to be reported under *Government Auditing Standards* or OMB Bulletin No. 14-02.

Management's Responsibility for Internal Control and Compliance

USOGE's management is responsible for (1) evaluating effectiveness of internal control over financial reporting based on criteria established under the Federal Managers Financial Integrity Act (FMFIA), (2) providing a statement of assurance on the overall effectiveness of internal control over financial reporting, (3) ensuring USOGE's financial management systems are in substantial compliance with FFMIA requirements, and (4) ensuring compliance with other applicable laws and regulations.

Auditor's Responsibilities

We are responsible for: (1) obtaining a sufficient understanding of internal controls over financial reporting to plan the audit, (2) testing compliance with certain provisions of laws and regulations that have a direct and material effect on the financial statements and applicable laws for which OMB Bulletin 14-02 requires testing, and (3) applying certain limited procedures with respect to the MD&A and other RSI.

We did not evaluate all internal controls relevant to operating objectives as broadly established by the FMFIA, such as those controls relevant to preparing statistical reports and ensuring efficient operations. We limited our internal control testing to testing controls over financial reporting. Because of inherent limitations in internal control, misstatements due to error or fraud, losses, or noncompliance may nevertheless occur and not be detected. We also caution that projecting our audit results to future periods is subject to risk that controls may become inadequate because of changes in conditions or that the degree of compliance with controls may deteriorate. In addition, we caution that our internal control testing may not be sufficient for other purposes.

We did not test compliance with all laws and regulations applicable to USOGE. We limited our tests of compliance to certain provisions of laws and regulations that have a direct and material effect on the financial statements and those required by OMB Bulletin 14-02 that we deemed applicable to USOGE's financial statements for the fiscal year ended September 30, 2013. We caution that noncompliance with laws and regulations may occur and not be detected by these tests and that such testing may not be sufficient for other purposes.

Purpose of the Report on Internal Control over Financial Reporting and the Report on Compliance and Other Matters

The purpose of the Report on Internal Control over Financial Reporting and the Report on Compliance and Other Matters sections of this report is solely to describe the scope of our testing of internal control and compliance and the result of that testing, and not to provide an opinion on the effectiveness of USOGE's internal control or on compliance. These reports are an integral part of an audit performed in accordance with Government Auditing Standards in considering USOGE's internal control and compliance. Accordingly, these reports are not suitable for any other purpose.

This report is intended solely for the information and use of the management of USOGE, OMB, and Congress, and is not intended to be and should not be used by anyone other than these specified parties.

Bean & Company

Largo, Maryland
December 11, 2013

UNITED STATES OFFICE OF GOVERNMENT ETHICS
BALANCE SHEET
AS OF SEPTEMBER 30, 2013 AND 2012
(In Dollars)

	2013	2012
Assets:		
Intragovernmental		
Fund Balance With Treasury (Note 2)	$ 4,996,548	$ 2,461,083
Accounts Receivable (Note 3)	108,244	53,371
Total Intragovernmental	5,104,792	2,514,454
Accounts Receivable, Net (Note 3)	141	352
Property, Equipment, and Software, Net (Note 4)	719,411	575,734
Total Assets	$ 5,824,344	$ 3,090,540
Liabilities:		
Intragovernmental		
Accounts Payable	$ 194,162	$ 458,465
Other (Note 7)	116,894	194,110
Total Intragovernmental	311,056	652,575
Accounts Payable	27,662	119,689
Federal Employee and Veterans' Benefits (Note 6)	412,377	401,523
Other (Note 7)	902,642	1,254,880
Total Liabilities (Note 5)	$ 1,653,737	$ 2,428,667
Net Position:		
Unexpended Appropriations - Other Funds	$ 4,656,283	$ 1,293,834
Cumulative Results of Operations - Other Funds	(485,676)	(631,961)
Total Net Position	$ 4,170,607	$ 661,873
Total Liabilities and Net Position	$ 5,824,344	$ 3,090,540

UNITED STATES OFFICE OF GOVERNMENT ETHICS
STATEMENT OF NET COST
FOR THE FISCAL YEARS ENDING SEPTEMBER 30, 2013 AND 2012
(In Dollars)

		2013		2012
Program Costs: (Note 9)				
Salaries and Expenses				
Gross Costs	$	14,905,188	$	14,540,418
Less: Earned Revenue		(143,443)		(505,711)
Net Cost of Operations	$	14,761,745	$	14,034,707

UNITED STATES OFFICE OF GOVERNMENT ETHICS
STATEMENT OF CHANGES IN NET POSITION
FOR THE FISCAL YEARS ENDING SEPTEMBER 30, 2013 AND 2012
(In Dollars)

	2013	2012
Cumulative Results of Operations:		
Beginning Balances	$ (631,961)	$ (908,040)
Budgetary Financing Sources:		
Appropriations Used	14,327,643	13,701,202
Imputed Financing Sources (Note 10)	580,387	609,584
Total Financing Sources	14,908,030	14,310,786
Net Cost of Operations	(14,761,745)	(14,034,707)
Net Change	146,285	276,079
Cumulative Results of Operations	$ (485,676)	$ (631,961)
Unexpended Appropriations:		
Beginning Balances	$ 1,293,834	$ 1,567,097
Budgetary Financing Sources:		
Appropriations Received	18,664,000	13,664,000
Other Adjustments	(973,908)	(236,061)
Appropriations Used	(14,327,643)	(13,701,202)
Total Budgetary Financing Sources	3,362,449	(273,263)
Total Unexpended Appropriations	$ 4,656,283	$ 1,293,834
Net Position	$ 4,170,607	$ 661,873

UNITED STATES OFFICE OF GOVERNMENT ETHICS
STATEMENT OF BUDGETARY RESOURCES
FOR THE FISCAL YEARS ENDING SEPTEMBER 30, 2013 AND 2012
(In Dollars)

	2013	2012
Budgetary Resources:		
	$	$
Unobligated Balance Brought Forward, October 1	452,333	533,611
Recoveries of Prior Year Unpaid Obligations	109,354	63,310
Other changes in unobligated balance	(3,380)	(236,060)
Unobligated balance from prior year budget authority, net	558,307	360,861
Appropriations	17,693,472	13,664,000
Spending authority from offsetting collections	172,857	484,581
	$	$
Total Budgetary Resources	18,424,636	14,509,442
Status of Budgetary Resources:		
	$	$
Obligations Incurred (Note 12)	18,000,752	14,057,109
Unobligated balance, end of year:		
Apportioned (Note 2)	81,357	200,306
Unapportioned (Note 2)	342,527	252,027
Total unobligated balance, end of year	423,884	452,333
	$	$
Total Budgetary Resources	18,424,636	14,509,442
Change in Obligated Balance		
Unpaid Obligations:		
	$	$
Unpaid Obligations, Brought Forward, October 1	2,110,447	2,553,021
Obligations Incurred (Note 12)	18,000,752	14,057,109
Outlays (gross)	(15,279,492)	(14,436,372)
Recoveries of Prior Year Unpaid Obligations	(109,354)	(63,310)
Unpaid Obligations, End of Year (Gross)	4,722,353	2,110,447
Uncollected payments:		
Uncollected Customer Payments, Federal Sources, Brought Forward, October 1	(101,697)	(86,677)

Change in Uncollected Customer Payments, Federal Sources	(47,992)	(15,021)
Uncollected Customer Payments, Federal Sources, End of Year	(149,689)	(101,697)
Obligated Balance, End of Year (Note 2)	$ 4,572,664	$ 2,008,750

Budget Authority and Outlays, Net:

Budget authority, gross	$ 17,866,329	$ 14,148,581
Actual offsetting collections	(124,865)	(469,560)
Change in uncollected customer payments from Federal sources	(47,992)	(15,021)
Budget Authority, net	$ 17,693,472	$ 13,664,000
Outlays, gross	$ 15,279,492	$ 14,436,372
Actual offsetting collections	(124,865)	(469,560)

NOTE 1. SUMMARY OF SIGNIFICANT ACCOUNTING POLICIES

A. Reporting Entity

The United States Office of Government Ethics (OGE) was established by the Ethics in Government Act of 1978. To carry out its leadership and oversight responsibilities over the executive branch ethics program, OGE promulgates and maintains enforceable standards of ethical conduct for approximately 2.7 million civilian employees in over 130 executive branch agencies and the White House; oversees a financial disclosure system that reaches more than 28,000 public and 325,000 confidential financial disclosure report filers; ensures that executive branch ethics programs are in compliance with applicable ethics laws and regulations; provides education and training to the more than 5,600 ethics officials executive branch-wide; conducts outreach to the general public, the private sector, and civil society; and shares model practices with state, local, and foreign governments, and international organizations.

OGE's greatest resource is its multi-disciplinary staff of attorneys, ethics and financial experts, and support staff. OGE is a lean organization, with approximately 80 full-time equivalents, and accomplishes its responsibilities by organizing cross-functional teams to perform such diverse tasks as working with Presidential nominees for appointments requiring Senate confirmation to resolve potential financial conflicts of interest, training executive branch ethics officials, and enhancing oversight of executive branch ethics programs.

General Funds are accounts used to record financial transactions arising under congressional appropriations or other authorizations to spend general revenues. General Fund Miscellaneous Receipts are accounts established for receipts of non-recurring activity, such as fines, penalties, fees and other miscellaneous receipts for services and benefits.

OGE has rights and ownership of all assets reported in these financial statements. OGE does not possess any non-entity assets.

B. Basis of Presentation

The financial statements have been prepared to report the financial position and results of operations of OGE. The Balance Sheet presents the financial position of the agency. The Statement of Net Cost presents the agency's operating results; the Statement of Changes in Net Position displays the changes in the agency's equity accounts. The Statement of Budgetary Resources presents the sources, status, and uses of the agency's resources and follows the rules for the Budget of the United States Government.

The statements are a requirement of the Chief Financial Officers Act of 1990, the Government Management Reform Act of 1994 and the Accountability of Tax Dollars Act of 2002. They have been prepared from, and are fully supported by, the books and records of OGE in accordance with the hierarchy of accounting principles generally accepted in the United States of America, standards issued by the Federal Accounting Standards Advisory Board (FASAB), Office of Management and Budget (OMB) Circular A-136, *Financial Reporting Requirements,* as amended, and OGE accounting policies which are summarized in this note. These statements, with the exception of the Statement of Budgetary Resources, are different from financial management reports, which are also prepared pursuant to OMB directives that are used to monitor and control OGE's use of budgetary resources. The financial statements and associated notes are presented on a comparative basis. Unless specified otherwise, all amounts are presented in dollars.

C. Basis of Accounting

Transactions are recorded on both an accrual accounting basis and a budgetary basis. Under the accrual method, revenues are recognized when earned, and expenses are recognized when a liability is incurred, without regard to receipt or payment of cash. Budgetary accounting facilitates compliance with legal requirements on the use of federal funds.

D. Fund Balance with Treasury

Fund Balance with Treasury is the aggregate amount of the OGE's funds with Treasury in expenditure, receipt, and revolving fund accounts. Appropriated funds recorded in expenditure accounts are available to pay current liabilities and finance authorized purchases.

OGE does not maintain bank accounts of its own, has no disbursing authority, and does not maintain cash held outside of Treasury. Treasury disburses funds for the agency on demand.

E. Accounts Receivable

Accounts receivable consists of amounts owed to OGE by other Federal agencies and the general public. Amounts due from Federal agencies are considered fully collectible. Accounts receivable from the public include reimbursements from employees. An allowance for uncollectible accounts receivable from the public is established when, based upon a review of outstanding accounts and the failure of all collection efforts, management determines that collection is unlikely to occur considering the debtor's ability to pay.

F. Property, Equipment, and Software

Property, equipment and software represent furniture, fixtures, equipment, and information technology hardware and software which are recorded at original acquisition cost and are depreciated or amortized using the straight-line method over their estimated useful lives. Major alterations and renovations are capitalized, while maintenance and repair costs are expensed as incurred. OGE's capitalization threshold is $50,000 for individual purchases and $500,000 for bulk purchases. Property, equipment, and software acquisitions that do not meet the capitalization criteria are expensed upon receipt. Applicable standard governmental guidelines regulate the disposal and convertibility of agency property, equipment, and software. The useful life classifications for capitalized assets are as follows:

Description	Useful Life (years)
Leasehold Improvements	9
Office Furniture	5
Computer Equipment	3
Office Equipment	5
Software	5

G. Advances and Prepaid Charges

Advance payments are generally prohibited by law. There are some exceptions, such as reimbursable agreements, subscriptions and payments to contractors and employees. Payments made in advance of the receipt of goods and services are recorded as advances or prepaid charges at the time of prepayment and recognized as expenses when the related goods and services are received.

H. Liabilities

Liabilities represent the amount of funds likely to be paid by OGE as a result of transactions or events that have already occurred.

OGE reports its liabilities under two categories, Intragovernmental and With the Public. Intragovernmental liabilities represent funds owed to another government agency. Liabilities with the Public represent funds owed to any entity or person that is not a federal agency, including private sector firms and federal employees. Each of these categories may include liabilities that are covered by budgetary resources and liabilities not covered by budgetary resources.

Liabilities covered by budgetary resources are liabilities funded by a current appropriation or other funding source. These consist of accounts payable and accrued payroll and benefits. Accounts payable represent amounts owed to another entity for goods ordered and received and for services rendered except for employees. Accrued payroll and benefits represent payroll costs earned by employees during the fiscal year which are not paid until the next fiscal year.

Liabilities not covered by budgetary resources are liabilities that are not funded by any current appropriation or other funding source. These liabilities consist of accrued annual leave, and actuarial FECA,

I. Annual, Sick, and Other Leave

Annual leave is accrued as it is earned, and the accrual is reduced as leave is taken. The balance in the accrued leave account is adjusted to reflect current pay rates. Liabilities associated with other types of vested leave, including compensatory, restored leave, and sick leave in certain circumstances, are accrued at year-end, based on latest pay rates and unused hours of leave. Funding will be obtained from future financing sources to the extent that current or prior year appropriations are not available to fund annual and other types of vested leave earned but not taken. Nonvested leave is expensed when used. Any liability for sick leave that is accrued but not taken by a Civil Service Retirement System (CSRS)-covered employee is transferred to the Office of Personnel Management (OPM) upon the retirement of that individual. Credit is given for sick leave balances in the computation of annuities upon the retirement of Federal Employees Retirement System (FERS)-covered employees effective at 50% beginning FY 2012 and 100% in 2014.

J. Accrued and Actuarial Workers' Compensation

The Federal Employees' Compensation Act (FECA) administered by the U.S. Department of Labor (DOL) addresses all claims brought by OGE employees for on-the-job injuries. The DOL bills each agency annually as its claims are paid, but payment of these bills is deferred for two years to allow for funding through the budget process. Similarly, employees that OGE terminates without cause may receive unemployment compensation benefits under the unemployment insurance program also administered by the DOL, which bills each agency quarterly for paid claims. Future appropriations will be used for the reimbursement to DOL. The liability consists of (1) the net present value of estimated future payments calculated by the DOL, and (2) the unreimbursed cost paid by DOL for compensation to recipients under the FECA.

K. Retirement Plans

OGE employees participate in either the CSRS or the FERS. The employees who participate in CSRS are beneficiaries of matching contribution, equal to seven percent of pay, distributed to their annuity account in the Civil Service Retirement and Disability Fund.

Prior to December 31, 1983, all employees were covered under the CSRS program. From January 1, 1984 through December 31, 1986, employees had the option of remaining under CSRS or joining FERS and Social Security. Employees hired as of January 1, 1987 are automatically covered by the FERS program. Both CSRS and FERS employees may participate in the federal Thrift Savings Plan (TSP). FERS employees receive an automatic agency contribution equal to one percent of pay and OGE matches any employee contribution up to an additional four percent of pay. For FERS participants, OGE also contributes the employer's matching share of Social Security.

FERS employees and certain CSRS reinstatement employees are eligible to participate in the Social Security program after retirement. In these instances, OGE remits the employer's share of the required contribution.

OGE recognizes the imputed cost of pension and other retirement benefits during the employees' active years of service. OPM actuaries determine pension cost factors by calculating the value of pension benefits expected to be paid in the future and communicate these factors to OGE for current period expense reporting. OPM also provides information regarding the full cost of health and life insurance benefits. OGE recognized the offsetting revenue as imputed financing sources to the extent these expenses will be paid by OPM.

OGE does not report on its financial statements information pertaining to the retirement plans covering its employees. Reporting amounts such as plan assets, accumulated plan benefits, and related unfunded liabilities, if any, is the responsibility of the OPM, as the administrator.

L. Other Post-Employment Benefits

OGE employees eligible to participate in the Federal Employees' Health Benefits Plan (FEHBP) and the Federal Employees' Group Life Insurance Program (FEGLIP) may continue to participate in these programs after their retirement. The OPM has provided OGE with certain cost factors that estimate the true cost of providing the post-retirement benefit to current employees. OGE recognizes a current cost for these and Other Retirement Benefits (ORB) at the time the employee's services are rendered. The ORB expense is financed by OPM, and offset by OGE through the recognition of an imputed financing source.

M. Use of Estimates

The preparation of the accompanying financial statements in accordance with generally accepted accounting principles requires management to make certain estimates and assumptions that affect the reported amounts of assets, liabilities, revenues, and expenses. Actual results could differ from those estimates.

N. Imputed Costs/Financing Sources

Federal Government entities often receive goods and services from other Federal Government entities without reimbursing the providing entity for all the related costs. In addition, Federal Government entities also incur costs that are paid in total or in part by other entities. An imputed financing source is recognized by the receiving entity for costs that are paid by other entities. OGE recognized imputed costs and financing sources in fiscal years 2013 and 2012 to the extent directed by accounting standards.

O. Reclassification

Certain fiscal year 2012 balances have been reclassified, retitled, or combined with other financial statement line items for consistency with the current year presentation.

NOTE 2. FUND BALANCE WITH TREASURY

Fund balance with Treasury account balances as of September 30, 2013 and 2012, were as follows:

		2013		2012
Fund Balances:				
Appropriated Funds	$	4,996,548	$	2,461,083
Total	$	4,996,548	$	2,461,083
Status of Fund Balance with Treasury:				
Unobligated Balance				
Available	$	81,357	$	200,306
Unavailable		342,527		252,027
Obligated Balance Not Yet Disbursed		4,572,664		2,008,750
Total	$	4,996,548	$	2,461,083

No discrepancies exist between the Fund Balance reflected on the Balance Sheet and the balances in the Treasury accounts.

The available unobligated fund balances represent the current-period amount available for obligation or commitment. At the start of the next fiscal year, this amount will become part of the unavailable balance as described in the following paragraph.

The unavailable unobligated fund balances represent the amount of appropriations for which the period of availability for obligation has expired. These balances are available for upward adjustments of obligations incurred only during the period for which the appropriation was available for obligation or for paying claims attributable to the appropriations.

The obligated balance not yet disbursed includes accounts payable, accrued expenses, and undelivered orders that have reduced unexpended appropriations but have not yet decreased the fund balance on hand (see also Note 13).

NOTE 3. ACCOUNTS RECEIVABLE

Accounts receivable balances as of September 30, 2013 and 2012, were as follows:

	2013	2012
Intragovernmental		
Accounts Receivable	$ 108,244	$ 53,371
Total Intragovernmental Accounts Receivable	$ 108,244	$ 53,371
With the Public		
Accounts Receivable	$ 141	$ 352
Total Accounts Receivable	$ 108,385	$ 53,723

The accounts receivable is primarily made up of receivables related to reimbursable activities.

Historical experience has indicated that the majority of the receivables are collectible. There are no material uncollectible accounts as of September 30, 2013 and 2012.

NOTE 4. PROPERTY, EQUIPMENT, AND SOFTWARE

Schedule of Property, Equipment, and Software as of September, 30, 2013

Major Class	Acquisition Cost	Accumulated Amortization/ Depreciation	Net Book Value
Software-in-Development	$ 719,411	$ -	$ 719,411
Total	$ 719,411	$ -	$ 719,411

Schedule of Property, Equipment, and Software as of September 30, 2012

Major Class	Acquisition Cost	Accumulated Amortization/ Depreciation	Net Book Value
Software-in-Development	$ 575,734	$ -	$ 575,734
Total	$ 575,734	$ -	$ 575,734

NOTE 5. LIABILITIES NOT COVERED BY BUDGETARY RESOURCES

The liabilities for OGE as of September 30, 2013 and 2012, include liabilities not covered by budgetary resources. Congressional action is needed before budgetary resources can be provided. Although future appropriations to fund these liabilities are likely and anticipated, it is not certain that appropriations will be enacted to fund these liabilities.

	2013		2012
Intragovernmental – FECA	$ 76,818	$	78,289
Intragovernmental – Unemployment Insurance	-		12,341
Unfunded Leave	717,166		729,341
Actuarial FECA	412,377		401,523
Total Liabilities Not Covered by Budgetary Resources	$ 1,206,361	$	1,221,494
Total Liabilities Covered by Budgetary Resources	447,376		1,207,173
Total Liabilities	$ 1,653,737	$	2,428,667

FECA liabilities represent the unfunded liability for actual workers compensation claims paid on OGE's behalf and payable to the DOL. OGE also records an actuarial liability for future workers compensation claims based on the liability to benefits paid (LBP) ratio provided by DOL and multiplied by the average of benefits paid over three years.

Unfunded leave represents a liability for earned leave and is reduced when leave is taken. The balance in the accrued annual leave account is reviewed quarterly and adjusted as needed to accurately reflect the liability at current pay rates and leave balances. Accrued annual leave is paid from future funding sources and, accordingly, is reflected as a liability not covered by budgetary resources. Sick and other leave is expensed as taken.

NOTE 6. ACTUARIAL FECA LIABILITY

FECA provides income and medical cost protection to covered federal civilian employees harmed on the job or who have contracted an occupational disease, and beneficiaries of employees whose death is attributable to a job-related injury or occupational disease. Claims incurred for benefits under FECA for OGE's employees are administered by the DOL and ultimately paid by OGE when funding becomes available.

OGE bases its estimate for FECA actuarial liability on the DOL's FECA model. The DOL method of determining the liability uses historical benefits payment patterns for a specific incurred period to predict the ultimate payments for the period. Based on the information provided by the DOL, OGE's liability as of September 30, 2013 and 2012, was $412,377 and $401,523 respectively.

NOTE 7. OTHER LIABILITIES

Other liabilities account balances as of September 30, 2013 were as follows:

	Current		Non Current		Total	
Intragovernmental						
FECA Liability	$	34,538	$	42,280	$	76,817
Payroll Taxes Payable		40,077		-		40,077
Total Intragovernmental Other Liabilities	$	74,615	$	42,280	$	116,894
With the Public						
Payroll Taxes Payable	$	6,852	$	-	$	6,852
Accrued Funded Payroll and Leave		178,623		-		178,623
Unfunded Leave		717,167		-		717,167
Total Public Other Liabilities	$	902,642	$	-	$	902,642

Other liabilities account balances as of September 30, 2012 were as follows:

	Current		Non Current		Total	
Intragovernmental						
FECA Liability	$	42,775	$	35,514	$	78,289
Unemployment Insurance Liability		12,340		-		12,340
Payroll Taxes Payable		103,481		-		103,481
Total Intragovernmental Other Liabilities	$	158,596	$	35,514	$	194,110
With the Public						
Payroll Taxes Payable	$	16,150	$	-	$	16,150
Accrued Funded Payroll and Leave		509,387		-		509,387
Unfunded Leave		729,343		-		729,343
Total Public Other Liabilities	$	1,254,880	$	-	$	1,254,880

NOTE 8. LEASES

Operating Leases

OGE occupies office space under a lease agreement that is accounted for as an operating lease. The lease term is for a period of ten (10) years commencing on February 2, 2004 and ends February 1, 2014:

Operating Lease:

Fiscal Year	Office Space
2014	$ 478,711
Total Future Payments	$ 478,711

The operating lease amount does not include estimated payments for leases with annual renewal options.

NOTE 9. INTRAGOVERNMENTAL COSTS AND EXCHANGE REVENUE

Intragovernmental costs and revenue represent exchange transactions between OGE and other federal government entities, and are in contrast to those with non-federal entities (the public). Such costs and revenue are summarized as follows:

	2013	2012
Program Costs		
Intragovernmental Costs	$ 5,361,483	$ 5,168,336
Public Costs	9,389,244	9,372,082
Total Program Costs	$ 14,750,727	$ 14,540,418
Intragovernmental Earned Revenue	(107,027)	(491,925)
Public Earned Revenue	(36,416)	(13,786)
Net Program Costs	$ 14,607,284	$ 14,034,707

NOTE 10. IMPUTED FINANCING SOURCES

OGE recognizes as imputed financing the amount of accrued pension and post-retirement benefit expenses for current employees. The assets and liabilities associated with such benefits are the responsibility of the administering agency, OPM. For the year ended September 30, 2013 and 2012, imputed financing was $425,926 and $609,584 respectively

NOTE 11. BUDGETARY RESOURCE COMPARISONS TO THE BUDGET OF THE UNITED STATES GOVERNMENT

The President's Budget that will include fiscal year 2013 actual budgetary execution information has not yet been published. The President's Budget is scheduled for publication in February 2014 and can be found at the OMB Web site: *http://www.whitehouse.gov/omb/*. The 2014 Budget of the United States Government, with the "Actual" column completed for 2012, has been reconciled to the Statement of Budgetary Resources and there were no material differences.

NOTE 12. APPORTIONMENT CATEGORIES OF OBLIGATIONS INCURRED

Obligations incurred and reported in the Statement of Budgetary Resources in 2013 and 2012 consisted of the following:

	2013	2012
Direct Obligations, Category A	$ 13,075,764	$ 13,563,869
Direct Obligations, Category B	4,740,000	-
Reimbursable Obligations, Category A	184,987	493,240
Total Obligations Incurred	$ 18,000,752	$ 14,057,109

Category A apportionments distribute budgetary resources by fiscal quarters.

Category B apportionments typically distribute budgetary resources by activities, projects, objects or a combination of these categories.

NOTE 13. UNDELIVERED ORDERS AT THE END OF THE PERIOD

For the fiscal years ended September 30, 2013 and 2012, budgetary resources obligated for undelivered orders amounted to $4,760,901 and $890,934, respectively.

NOTE 14. CUSTODIAL ACTIVITY

OGE's custodial collection primarily consists of Freedom of Information Act requests. While these collections are considered custodial, they are neither primary to the mission of OGE nor material to the overall financial statements. OGE's total custodial collections are $0 and $(663) for the years ended September 30, 2013, and 2012, respectively.

NOTE 15. RECONCILIATION OF NET COST OF OPERATIONS TO BUDGET

OGE has reconciled its budgetary obligations and non-budgetary resources available to its net cost of operations.

	2013	2012
Resources Used to Finance Activities:		
Budgetary Resources Obligated		
Obligations Incurred	$ 18,000,752	$ 14,057,109
Spending Authority From Offsetting Collections and Recoveries	(282,211)	(547,891)
Net Obligations	17,718,541	13,509,218
Other Resources		
Imputed Financing From Costs Absorbed By Others	425,926	609,584
Net Other Resources Used to Finance Activities	425,926	609,584
Total Resources Used to Finance Activities	18,144,467	14,118,802
Resources Used to Finance Items Not Part of the Net Cost of Operations	(3,548,250)	(110,168)
Total Resources Used to Finance the Net Cost of Operations	14,596,217	14,008,634
Components of the Net Cost of Operations That Will Not Require or Generate Resources in the Current Period:	11,067	26,073
Net Cost of Operations	$ 14,607,284	$ 14,034,707